Titles in this Series

The Story of
Peter Tchaikovsky

By

Opal Wheeler

Illustrated by Christine Price

The Story of Peter Tchaikovsky
Written by Opal Wheeler

Originally published by E.P. Dutton & Company, New York, 1953.
Copyright © 1953, by Opal Wheeler.

ISBN 978-1-61006-014-1
Copyright © 2011 by Zeezok Publishing, LLC
Published July, 2017
Printed in the United States of America

Zeezok Publishing, LLC
PO Box 1960 • Elyria, OH 44036
info@Zeezok.com • 1-800-749-1681

www.Zeezok.com

The Story of
Peter Tchaikovsky

CHAPTER ONE

"On Stardust! On Comet! On!"

The Cossack guardsmen, one hundred strong, urged their fiery steeds into the icy courtyard of their master, Ilya Tchaikovsky.

Strange to be called so early in the morning, with the May sun blinking sleepy red eyes at the bleak countryside. Raw and cold it was in the little mining town of Votkinsk, on the edge of Asia. Snow crystals glistened on rough cobbles and white drifts covered the land as far as the eye could see.

The horses pawed the ground and whinnied impatiently.

"Steady, boy!" The head rider pulled hard on the reins of his restless black stallion. "The master comes soon."

Hardly were the words spoken than the door of the great house swung open. The men wheeled to attention as mine-inspector Tchaikovsky looked swiftly over the fur-hatted group. A warm smile lighted his handsome face.

"My good men," said he, briskly, "You will rejoice with me to hear the news that I bring you. God has blessed us with a fair little son. We have already named him Peter Ilyich Tchaikovsky."

With a ringing shout, the men threw their caps high in the air.

"Peter Ilyich" Their calls echoed in the frosty morning. "Long life to Peter Ilyich Tchaikovsky!"

Around the courtyard they galloped at full speed, hoofs striking sparks on rough cobbles. At the deafening din, the household of servants ran to the windows to watch the gay parade.

Ilya Tchaikovsky laughed merrily and joined his two-year-old Nicholas indoors, whose short nose was pressed hard against the pane, eyes round at the spectacle outside.

"A fine salute to your new little brother, yes?" Father Tchaikovsky patted the small head and swung off for another look at the tiny newcomer.

No baby could have been born into a more loving household. Beautiful mother Tchaikovsky shook her head in dismay as aunts, uncles, cousins, and an army of servants hovered over him, obeying his every wish through the long bright months.

"Careful!" she cautioned. "We must not spoil this lovely child."

But it was difficult not to spoil elfin, blue-eyed Peter, who loved horses more than anything else in his small world. As soon as he could walk about on his short legs, straight to the courtyard he took himself.

"Midnight, come!" he called at the top of his voice to his father's favorite mount.

Ilya Tchaikovsky was amused at the small boy, looking so stern as he gave his command. But more surprised he was to see the great black animal moving slowly to the tiny hand for the big lump of sugar.

Each day, after seeing that all went well at the mines, Ilya hurried back home to find fair-haired Peter waiting patiently on the top step.

"Always ready for the ride," he chuckled, sweeping the little one to the saddle. "Away then, brave horseman. Away to the moon!"

With a shout of joy, Peter clutched the reins and slapped them with all his might, urging the steed to a gallop. Never was there fear in the bright eyes, no matter how fast the pace.

"Oho, a splendid rider we shall have," laughed Ilya, watching the flying locks and bright cheeks. "Some day you shall take charge of the men at the mines, my little Petia. Miles and miles you shall ride to your heart's content."

There was always a storm of tears when the gallop was at an end. No one could bring him comfort but his lovely mother.

"Come, little one, we shall have some music," she coaxed, wiping the small face with her perfumed kerchief.

The sounds were magic. To her sprightly, simple melodies at the piano, Peter and Nicholas flew to the center of the room, dancing as fast as their feet would go.

"More! More!" called Peter, the moment the music stopped.

Everyone gathered around, aunts, cousins, and servants, to watch the small boy, his face alight with joy. While weary Nicholas lay stretched on the floor, Peter tried the Russian dances, difficult, indeed, even for grownups.

"Bravo! Bravo!" called the audience, clapping and swaying to the merry tunes.

"It is enough now!" Mother Tchaikovsky left the piano, her fingers aching from playing the same melodies over and over again. "I declare, the child will be a dancer some day."

Ilya smiled and shook his head as the small performer climbed onto his knees to rest.

"A dancer? Never! The boy will be a horseman, perhaps an officer in the army some day."

His words seemed to be true. As he grew older, Peter spent more and more of his time with the animals in the barns. Whenever anyone called, "Peter, where are you?" someone was sure to answer, "Look in the stalls. You'll find him with the horses, no doubt."

The greatest day of his life was when Ilya gave him permission to ride alone in the parade at dusk. Mounted on a gentle little pony, Peter cantered to the head of the army of Cossack horsemen.

How the men laughed as the young rider sat with shoulders squared, head erect, shouting his commands with all his might.

"Left, wheel! Right, gallop!"

Nicholas and his small cousin, Lydia, clapped and waved their hands at the gay parade.

As soon as he was old enough, Peter joined the children in

all their games. Then what fine times there were, exploring the countryside and casting their hooks for fish in the shadowy little stream. In an old cave not far away, they played their favorite game of robbers until twilight brought them indoors. And there was berry-picking through drowsy summer mornings, when they wandered, singing, in the sweet smelling meadows. Peter's quick eyes always found the biggest patches of fruit, ripe and shining in the deep grasses.

"Come!" he would shout, swinging his pail over his head. "Come and pick in my patch!"

He was the first to fill his tin bucket and lead the little procession back home, a trusty servant following on guard.

What a feast there was beside the crackling fire in the great back kitchen, the big bowls of juicy berries topped with thick, sugared cream.

The good times went on until the morning when Fanny Durbach came all the way from France to live in the household and teach Nicholas and Lydia in the sunny schoolroom.

"Lessons, lessons!" sang Peter, twisting the buttons of his new red jacket. "We will all have lessons!"

"All but Petia," said his mother, gently. "You are too young to study, little one. But you will find plenty to do until the others have finished their work."

Peter was sad, indeed, and wandered off by himself. The whole world seemed suddenly strange and quiet, and he did not like the silence that settled over the big house like a heavy blanket. Lonelier than he had ever been in his four and a half years, he took himself to the stables. But everything was deserted. Even his good friend, the head boy, was nowhere to be seen.

Suddenly a low whinny sounded behind him, and turning quickly, he discovered the big black stallion that his father usually rode to the mines.

"Midnight!" Peter ran to the noble animal, standing near the gate at one end of the courtyard. "Why are you here, boy?"

He patted the sleek sides of his father's favorite horse and was rewarded with another soft whinny.

"We will go for a little ride, yes, Midnight?" Loosening the rope, Peter climbed up the fence and slid into the saddle. Slapping the reins gently, he urged the animal out onto the roadway.

What a beautiful day for a canter. Peter wrinkled his nose in the sun and thumped his small heels against the animal's sides.

"Lazybones!" he scolded. "Stretch your legs, fat Lazybones!"

Midnight tossed his mane and picked his way carefully over the slippery cobbles. Free of the outer buildings, he broke

into a slow trot. This was better than lessons! Peter shouted with glee and struck up a song that he had heard the servants sing when they were happy.

> "The missus is good, and the master brave,
> Now who could ask for more?
> Save the lovin' cup, let's mix 'er up
> And drink till the break o' day."

The young voice was clear and true, and a strange old man on the roadway stopped to listen.

"Where ye bound, young'un?" he inquired, resting on his stick cane.

"To the end of the world," shouted Peter. "THE VERY END OF THE WORLD. And when we get tired, we'll slide right home on the edge of a rainbow."

The old man smiled and slapped his knee.

"On a rainbow! Ah now, young'un, better go back to yer ma and pa. Storm comin' up yonder."

He pointed to the west where the angry clouds were pushing their heads into the sky. But Peter only laughed and dug his heels into Midnight's sides, urging him on to a faster pace. Again he broke into merry singing, this time of his own inventing.

> "On, Midnight, on Midnight,
>   On, on, on.
>   We'll ride and ride
>   Right into the sun.
>   And when we get tired, we'll ride some more,
>   Until we find we're at our door."

The road wound in and out, up hill and down again. Past workers in the field it wandered, and by little huts with lean children playing around the doorway.

Peter smiled and waved his hand. This was a great adventure, every turn bringing fresh sights and sounds. He sighed happily and went on with his singing.

Back in the Tchaikovsky home, lessons were at an end, and the new teacher smiled at her charges.

"A good beginning, my young pupils. Now you must have a big hunger for the lunch, yes? When we find the littlest one, we shall all be ready."

The children ran into the courtyard, shouting "Peter! Peter!" But there was no answer to their calls. High and low they searched, but he was nowhere to be found. Alarmed, the governess hurried to Mother Tchaikovsky's quarters at one end of the vast house.

"Madame, we cannot find the smallest child. He does not seem to be anywhere about," she explained.

"Peter? Ah well, he is playing one of his little tricks again. You will find him hidden away in one of his favorite spots."

"Oh no, Madame. The children and I have searched well."

A heavy clap of thunder roused Mother Tchaikovsky.

"He is fearful of storms," she declared, going quickly to the doorway. "We must find him at once, before it breaks."

"Peter! Peter! Peter!" The call rang in every part of the big house and echoed through the smaller buildings. But no voice came back in answer.

"Send for the master at once," ordered Mother Tchaikovsky, her face pale. "And sound the alarm to call the men."

The clanging of the great bell set up a fearful din. Soon hoof-beats clattered through the courtyard as Ilya galloped to the head of the group, a worried frown on his brow.

"The child must have gone off on Midnight!" he exclaimed. "But he could not have gone far on a lame animal. Forward, men! We will search the caves first."

The bodyguard set out at once, calling "Peter! Peter!" But only hollow echoes came back to answer them from the dark caverns.

The thunder was rolling heavily now, with forked lightning scratching through foaming clouds. From the leaden sky, heavy drops began to spatter the ground.

"To the roadway!" commanded Ilya. "We must find the child before the storm breaks in earnest."

Well he remembered the trembling little figure that ran to hide in the deepest closet whenever lightning or thunder told of a coming downpour.

Still another fear clutched at the heart of mine inspector Tchaikovsky. Many tales there were of the bands of harsh men roaming the countryside in search of an easy living. And so there was real need of the strong bodyguard of horsemen surrounding Ilya and his family at all times.

Down the road he galloped with the riders, urging his steed onward to a faster pace. Every nook and hamlet and meadow was searched with keen eyes, but Peter was nowhere to be seen.

A clap of thunder shook the ground and the rain began to fall in blinding sheets. Ilya pulled his hat down over his eyes. Rounding a sharp bend, he came upon a group of workmen seeking shelter under a tree.

"Have you seen a boy, very small, riding a black stallion?" he shouted above the storm.

"Sorry. No, master. We just came from your roadway, short time back."

Never did the miles seem so long. As they rode through a little thicket, Ilya turned to the guard at his side.

"Could the boy have gone so far?" he asked, his eyes dark with worry.

"Young master is an excellent rider for his years, sir. But we should come upon him at any moment now."

Up a steep hill they climbed slowly. At the top, one of the men was shouting and waving his arms.

"He is found, sir! Over there."

Ilya galloped at full speed to a heavy clump of trees. There in the saddle was a small figure, his head buried in the horse's mane, hands tight over his ears to shut out the fury of the storm.

Ilya lifted the rain-soaked child to his saddle and wrapped him snugly in his great cape. But the trembling did not stop, and from under the dark lashes, tears fell in a steady stream over the small, white cheeks. Father Tchaikovsky looked down at his son, burrowed like a rabbit against him.

"You are safe now, little one. But tell me, why did you go so far away?" he asked gently.

Slowly the blue eyes opened a crack.

"They would not let me have lessons. So I thought–I thought–" the voice trailed off in a whisper.

His father finished for him. "You thought you would go for a little ride."

There was great rejoicing at the big house on his safe return, and soon he was between warm blankets and far off in the land of dreams.

The next morning he was none the worse for his adventure, and skipping from his bed, he was the first one stirring in the household.

"Today I will have lessons with the others?" Peter's blue eyes searched his mother's lovely face.

At the pleading look, she nodded her head slowly.

"Though you have not earned the right, you may join the children." Looking at him more closely, she shook her head in dismay. "But a gentleman does not go to school with hair uncombed, shoes untied, and buttons off his new jacket."

Peter pushed his hair down quickly and bent to fasten his shoes.

"It is no use to bother," said he, looking back with a bright smile. "Tomorrow it will look the same when I get up."

Mother Tchaikovsky sighed as Fanny came into the room.

"Ah Mademoiselle, you will have much to do, I fear, in helping this little boy to be clean and tidy. And now Petia, see that you do not disturb the others in their work."

The new teacher put her arm around the young shoulders.

"He will be no trouble, Madame. And who knows, he may be able to keep up with his brother and cousin.

Little did she know how true her words would be. Not only was Peter able to do the lessons, but he was also the first to read in French and German, besides his own Russian language. But never could she tell what her youngest pupil would do next.

One grey morning, when she arrived in the schoolroom, she was startled at the sound of sharp blows. Whack! Whack!

Whack! Thump! Whack! There was her young pupil bending over a large map of the world, banging with his fist on all of the countries excepting his own.

"Why, Peter!" she exclaimed. "How could you be so unkind to the people of the whole world? All of those boys and girls say the same prayers as you. And even your own Fanny, who is French—you would hurt her, too!"

Peter listened, his eyes lowered for a moment. Then a merry smile chased away the frown.

"Oh, you do not need to scold me," said he. "Didn't you see me cover France with my hand first?"

How different was this child from the others, thought Fanny, as she watched the delicate little face. Many times he was unruly and deserved punishment. But the slightest words would bring a storm of tears that seemed never to end.

There he sat now, swinging his legs under the table, lost in dreams. His hair was on end and spots covered his short coat. Turning and twisting the poor buttons, they dropped one by one to the floor. Peter looked after them with a smile. It was such fun to see them go rolling away.

Fanny shook her head and sighed. Perhaps Mother

Tchaikovsky was right. She might never teach this child to be neat and tidy. That very morning, when she had coaxed him to take his bath with Nicholas, he had run away, calling back to her, "It would do no good, Fanny! I will be just as dirty again tomorrow!"

Peter's blue eyes brightened as he held up his copybook for his beloved teacher to see.

"Look, Fanny. I have finished a new poem about God caring for the animals. And I wrote it in French!"

"All by yourself!" exclaimed the governess, her motherly face beaming. "You shall read it for us this very minute."

Skipping to her chair, Peter leaned against the warm shoulder and was just beginning the lines when a shadow darkened the door.

"Father!" The children ran to the tall figure, all work forgotten.

"Come, come," he admonished them gently. "You are in school now. I have come to see how well you know your lessons."

"Then you shall hear my poem, Father!"

Peter rocked back and forth in delight, pulling on the last poor coat button as he recited the lines without looking at the paper.

Ilya sat quietly, listening in amazement. This child had a great gift, indeed.

"So, little Petia," he said at last. "First you would be a horseman, then a dancer, and now a poet!"

Fanny added quickly, "And the verses come without the boy's trying, sir. Here is his copybook, filled to overflowing, with his own drawings for decoration."

The master held out his hand. "I will take it with me, to see what this young mischief-maker has been up to."

He tucked the book under his arm and started for the door.

"There is a new pony down in the courtyard, Peter. He was brought in from the field this morning. Perhaps the others could do without you while you have a look at him."

"Oh, father!" With a shout of joy the young student was off in a flash for an hour of riding in the paddock.

Peter loved his home and everyone around him. The hours were filled to overflowing and evening came all too soon. But he shivered with delight when the simple meal was over and he heard the call, "Stories, Peter. Fanny is ready."

Into the small sitting room next to the bedroom, he raced with Nicholas and Lydia. There, before a bright fire, he listened with all his might to the rousing tales that Fanny read from a big book that she had brought all the way from France.

One evening, halfway through a story of adventure, she closed the book suddenly.

"Who would like to go on with the tale?" she asked, a curious smile lighting her calm, dark eyes.

"To make it up?" asked Nicholas.

Before there was time to reply, Peter sprang to his feet and began at once to finish the story.

> "It was a black, black night when the boat struck the rocks," he started. "The sea was roaring and the wind sent the waves high over the decks. 'We are lost,' shouted the men. 'We must make for the shore.' Into the cold waters they leaped together and swam and swam through the night. As morning dawned, they spied a piece of land far to the west."

On and on went the tale, the children hanging on every word. The young storyteller could not stop now, with such an audience, and after many exciting adventures, he let the yarn spin itself out.

"And at last they were dead, dead, dead!" he cried, his voice dying away to a whisper.

The young listeners' eyes were wide with wonder. "It's better than the real story!" they declared.

Fanny nodded. "Far better," she agreed. "So now we have Peter the horseman, the dancer, the poet, and the storyteller. But now to bed," she ordered, "Or tomorrow's lessons will suffer from sleepy-headed children."

Peter wakened early the next morning to find that his father had gone on a journey to the big city of St. Petersburg. It would be days before he would return, and Peter felt lonely, indeed. Not until the loving voice and gay laughter sounded through the rooms again, would he be truly happy.

Each day seemed longer than the one before, and often his mother came suddenly upon the quiet little figure sitting alone on the window ledge.

"Why do you not play games with the other children?" she questioned gently, patting the tousled locks into place.

Peter looked up, startled. "But I might miss father when he comes home!" he declared.

He had not many more days to wait. One afternoon, just as the sun was slipping from the plains, there was ringing laughter outside the door. Peter sped like an arrow across the polished floor and flung himself into the strong arms.

"Father! You stayed away so long! The dog has new puppies and my pony is sick and my hen won't lay eggs!"

Ilya roared with glee as the words tumbled out.

"The whole world has turned helter skelter in ten short days," he cried. Turning in the doorway he motioned to the men behind him. "Now for the fine surprise, my son. It has come all the way from St. Petersburg with me. Carefully, carefully!" he cautioned, as the men placed an enormous box on the floor.

Peter could scarcely wait for the heavy wrappings to be taken off. How could a surprise be so big?

The last packing was pulled loose, and there stood a tall, shiny brown box. With a pleased smile, father Tchaikovsky pulled a little lever at the top and the room was filled with the most beautiful music.

Peter stood without moving, his eyes fastened on the machine. Never had he heard such lovely sounds, his whole life long. His breath came faster and faster, until he felt something would burst inside him.

Suddenly he began to run around the instrument, clapping his hands and laughing at the top of his voice. Then, stopping short, he put his arms around the box and laid his head against the shiny wood. Tears splashed down his cheeks and sobs shook him from head to toe.

"Petia! Little Petia! You like the music box so much, then." Ilya's arms were around the trembling shoulders. "It is a very fine instrument, my son. I know that you will take good care of it, so that it will bring you joy for long years to come."

From that moment on, except for lessons, Peter would not leave the orchestrion. The beautiful works of some of the greatest composers, Bellini and Donizetti and Mozart, he was hearing for the first time. Many, many pieces there were, played by a fine orchestra. Of them all, he loved the music of Mozart best.

At night he could not sleep for thinking of the singing melodies. Often, creeping down the slippery stairs in the darkness, he would start the music box. With knees under his chin, he sat in a little round ball, his head against his beloved orchestrion as he drank in every glorious sound.

"Peter! Peter!" There was Fanny, calling softly in the hallway above. "This is no time for music! Come to bed at once!"

A small voice answered her at last.

"The angels are singing to me, Fanny. I can't go now. "

"Tomorrow they will sing even more beautifully," the calm, gentle voice assured him. "Come, little one. We will dream about the lovely melodies until the stars fade away."

But Peter's hunger was never satisfied. Now, as soon as he knew a melody by heart, off he raced to the piano. Over and over he worked until he could play it without a single mistake. When it was to his liking, he would sigh with delight and run back to the beloved music box to hear it all over again.

One morning as he stood at the window, lost to everything

but the new, galloping music on the orchestrion, he began to tap on the pane in time to the stirring rhythm. Thumpity-thump. Thumpity-thump.

Faster and faster, louder and louder went the music, and in Peter's mind, a picture began to grow. Yes, that was it! Five hundred, six hundred, seven hundred mighty warriors were charging up a hill. On the fiercest stallion of all, he was leading the brigade.

Thumpity-thump. Thumpity-thump. Peter's hands beat harder on the pane as the thundering hooves roared over the top. Victory at last!

Thumpity-thump. CRASH. The window broke into a thousand pieces, flying glass clattering over the polished floor.

Cries and running footsteps came from all parts of the house.

"Petia! Petia! Are you hurt?" In a frenzy, Mother Tchaikovsky examined the small, bleeding hands. Ilya was on his knees, trying to help.

"Thank heaven, there is not much harm done," said he, holding the bandages as Mother Tchaikovsky bound up the throbbing fingers.

"Tell us, child, what were you doing?"

Peter looked into the anxious faces gathered around him.

"Why—it was just the music. And the horses were galloping to the music," he tried to explain.

There was silence for a moment as his father looked at Mother Tchaikovsky.

"Music, music, music!" Ilya said the words slowly. "Perhaps we had better find someone to teach the boy, so that he will have enough of it, once and for all. Yes, perhaps that is the secret."

Peter was listening with all his might.

"The secret!" he cried, waving his bandaged hands in air. "The secret is music!"

CHAPTER TWO

A golden shaft of sunlight stole into the large sleeping room of the children. Slowly it crept from square to square along the highly-polished floor. Peeping slyly through a slit in the heavy curtains, it wakened Peter from a sound sleep.

"Time to get ready for the party!" he announced, bounding like a rabbit through the long halls. "It's party day!"

"Sh! Peter!" Fanny darted after him in her grey dressing gown. "Quiet, little rascal! The mother and father still sleep!"

But the mischief had already been done. Who could rest in such a noisy din? And indeed it was time to be stirring, with so much to be done for the evening celebration.

Soon the household was bustling with preparations for the yearly gathering in the large home of the Tchaikovskys. Peter was in the midst of all the excitement. Upstairs and downstairs he flew, putting the chairs in neat rows. In and out of the kitchens he darted to watch the cakes spreading over the shelves and sniff the meats sizzling and browning in the great ovens. Munching a poppyseed tart, he peered cautiously into the bubbling soup kettle.

"Begone with you, child!" scolded the chief cook, playfully swooping down on him with a long ladle. "Begone, or there'll be no appetite for the banquet."

At last all was in readiness as darkness fell softly over the little mining town of Votkinsk. In his new suit, Peter watched the guests arrive. He clapped and cried out with joy when the fireworks were set off in the courtyard, the blazing colors spinning dizzily in the night sky.

The groaning tables called the guests indoors, and when the feasting was ended, the music began. This was the time that Peter had longed for. Leaning against the piano, he watched

his mother's fingers move swiftly over the keys as she played for the dancing.

Round and round, over the polished floor glided the stately couples. A burst of applause rewarded mother Tchaikovsky for her efforts, and she left the instrument to speak for a moment with her guests.

Peter looked swiftly around the room. This was his chance to help with the evening's entertainment! Slipping into the chair left by his mother, he began to play one of the Mozart melodies from the music box.

As the lovely music stole into the room, the talking stopped. In surprise the guests turned to watch the small boy on the high bench as his fingers flew over the keys in a rollicking caprice of the great master.

Peter was completely lost in the music. Not a single note did he forget, and not once did he stumble as he played on and on through the difficult composition.

"A true musician! How long has the boy been playing? Where have you been hiding this fine pianist?" the questions ran around the great room.

Mother and father Tchaikovsky listened with a smile.

"Oh, the child amuses himself with his melodies, it is true. He has surprised us with playing for so large an audience." Laughingly, Mother Tchaikovsky took her place again at the piano. "On with the dancing, my good friends," she called gaily.

As her fingers ran over the keys, her eyes swept the room searchingly, but no Peter was to be seen. Where could he have gone so quickly? A moment later she looked up in surprise to find Fanny standing anxiously at her elbow.

"It is the little one, Madame. Perhaps you had better come. I can do nothing with him."

Mother Tchaikovsky left the piano at once and hurried up the long staircase. Near the door of the children's room she heard a wailing cry.

"Save me! Save me, Fanny! They will not let me alone!"

There sat Peter, bolt upright, his eyes staring, cheeks red as he beat the covers with his fist.

Mother Tchaikovsky laid her hand gently on the hot forehead.

"What is it, small one?" she asked quietly. "Tell us what troubles you so sorely."

Peter stared up at her, eyes wide.

"The music!" he shouted. "The music will not let me go! Save me from the melodies!" His hand flew to his head. "They are here! The music will not stop!"

His mother sat beside the trembling figure, speaking in low, comforting tones.

"Hearken, my dear little Petia, Fanny and I will chase them all away. Now they are flying from the window, to sail far out on the clouds, over the starlit meadows to St. Petersburg."

At last he fell into a troubled sleep, and Mother Tchaikovsky left the faithful Fanny to keep watch as she hurried below to her guests.

Late that night, when the last carriage had rolled away, she talked long with her husband.

"Ah yes, we must take great care, indeed," sighed Ilya. "Music excites the boy too strongly. Strange that he must have it to be happy." He sighed again. "A problem. We must warn the new teacher not to let him have too much at a time."

But the lessons with Marie Palchikov delighted the young student. Never could he hear enough of her music. The works of many new masters she played for him, and after listening carefully, Peter sat at the keyboard to play bits of the melodies, exactly as she had done.

Madame Palchikov could scarcely believe her ears. Here was a rare gift, indeed! But she must not spoil the boy.

"It is good to play what you hear, Peter," said she, watching the eager little face. "But it is far better to read the notes for yourself. Now then, to work!"

Indeed it was hard work, but not too much for the new pupil. Hours after his teacher had left, he still sat at the piano, struggling with the notes that stared at him from the pages. But what fun it was to master the difficult chore and hear for the first time the new music of the great composers.

Now, most of his time was spent at the instrument, and almost impossible it was to coax him away.

"Peter!" his father would call from the doorway. "Your pony needs a canter. Time to feed the chickens, son. Would you like to join the children for a picnic?"

But the answer was always the same.

"When the music is right, I will come."

As soon as he could play perfectly the work left him by his patient teacher, he tried out his own melody that was growing in his mind. This was best of all. Over and over he played the little tune, changing it here and there. Then slowly he added the other parts until the music was rich and full. When it was finished, off he raced to find Fanny.

"It is ready! Come!" he would cry, leading her back to the piano.

Fanny sat in a big chair close to the instrument, watching the flying fingers and the bright young face bent over the keys. So much beauty was here, and suffering, too. There would be much of it in his life, she told herself, sadly. If only she could be with him when things hurt him deeply, how happy she would be.

A loud crash startled her from her thoughts. Peter laughed gaily, hands in air.

"What did the music tell you, Fanny?" He questioned her eagerly.

When she did not answer at once, he laughed again and began to twist the front of his jacket.

"The buttons, Peter! Save the buttons!" cried the governess. "Ah yes, the crash in the music. I think it might have been the moon tumbling into the sea at midnight."

"Oh no, Fanny." Peter screwed his eyes shut. "It was a great army of hungry giants in bright red cloaks, stalking the forest in search of men to eat. Very bad they were, too. On they strode to a clearing where little children were playing. Smacking their lips, they were about to gobble them up when a clap of thunder opened the earth. Down, down, down they tumbled to the bottom of the hole with a terrible thud. And that was the end of the giants!"

Fanny smiled. Perhaps this would be a good time to get her charge away from the instrument.

"The very thing, Peter. Let's play giants!"

"Yes! Down in the caves!"

It was fun in the dusky caverns, and the children raced and called and played games to their hearts content. Peter led the group, his giant band lying in wait for the other, pouncing on the lair with loud cries.

The echoes were deafening, and poor Fanny clapped her hands to her ears. But the children were never happier and were sorry when it was time to leave their games and go indoors for bowls of hot soup before bedtime.

When he was eight years old, Peter could read music as well as his teacher, and Marie Palchikov stopped one day to speak with mother Tchaikovsky.

"There is little more that I can give your son, Madame," said she. "I would be sad to lose him, but it would be well, now, for him to have a new master."

Mother Tchaikovsky smiled and held out her hand.

"I give you our gracious thanks for all that you have done for Peter," said she, quietly. "It is just time to tell you that soon we shall be moving to St. Petersburg, where many new experiences will be awaiting our son. The music will be taken care of in some manner, you may be sure."

Peter could not believe his ears as his mother led his kind friend to the door. He would never see her again! Never would there be good times at the instrument that they both loved so well.

He stared hard at the floor as his mother's words echoed on in his mind. To leave the only home that he knew and loved with all his heart? And how could he part from his favorite pony, who would be watching each night for special tidbits before bedtime? But most of all, how could he bear to say farewell to Fanny, who had cared for him so faithfully for more than four long years?

Loneliness settled over him, deeper than any he had ever known.

Mother Tchaikovsky came again to the room and looked quietly at the unhappy face.

"You will surely like the big city, my son. There will be many new things for you to do," said she, gently. "And it will be fine to have a new home."

Peter sprang to his feet, his face white.

"But I do not need a new home!" he shouted, his fists clenched. "This is my home. I will not leave my home!"

His mother came toward him. "Ah yes, child. A good home it has been, and you have been happy here. But most of all, it is time for you to go to a big school with other boys."

Peter looked at her in dismay. "There is Fanny. She teaches me what I need to know."

Suddenly he rushed from the room, shouting, "I will not go away! This is my home!"

Out to the stables he ran, to bury his face in his pony's mane. "Lightfoot! Lightfoot! How could I ever leave you!"

The hot tears rained down the little animal's neck, and a soft whinny only made them fall the faster.

Through the days Peter roamed about silently, visiting the places he loved best. When the packing began, he watched quietly, making no outcry when his own belongings were put away in great boxes.

Lessons went on in the morning hours, and he sat at the low table, head resting on his hands, saying not a word. His large blue eyes followed his beloved teacher wherever she moved.

A sharp pain struck at her as Fanny looked at her favorite pupil. If only she could help him to be happy again. If only she could go to St. Petersburg to live so that the lessons would not have to end.

At last the packing was finished and the day came for Fanny to leave the old house in Votkinsk. Sadly everyone in the household gathered around the carriage for a last farewell.

Mother Tchaikovsky looked quickly about her.

"Peter! Where is Peter?" she asked, a puzzled frown on her lovely brow. "Not a sign of him has there been this whole morning long."

"Peter! Peter!" The calls rang through the courtyard. But no voice came back to answer them.

There was no time to waste, and the driver cracked his whip.

"Please tell him farewell for me." Fanny leaned from the carriage and waved as the horses broke into a trot and carried her out onto the roadway. Looking up at the noonday sun, she sighed heavily. A beautiful day for the first part of her journey.

But sorely she missed seeing Peter and tucking the surprise box into his hand. There it lay in the dark stillness in her pocket, and she felt the little spring click when the carriage jolted on the sharp cobbles.

"Fair day for the ride, Miss," the driver called back over his shoulder. "Be arrivin' at the next station less than two hours. Fresh horses'll carry yer on while me and the boys git back to Votkinsk. Plenty ter do with family movin' ter Petersburg come mornin'. Now I says ter my missus, 'Too bad ter quit the quiet life at Votkinsk.' But my missus says, 'Them little ones, now, they must git larnin' in the big city,' she says. 'Larnin'? says I. 'Them little heads'll git filled with plenty o'larnin' right here in Votkinsk,' says I."

On and on went the rumbly voice. Would it never end? Fanny sighed and closed her eyes, thinking again of the boy who had not come to bid her farewell.

An hour passed by and the lively horses seemed not to tire of the fast pace as they trotted briskly along. Past farm houses and quiet meadows they whirled. From a little church on a hill came the sound of singing. Rich and full and hearty were the tones, and Fanny leaned from the carriage to listen.

How Peter would love the music, she thought. A wave of sadness swept over her. "Peter and his music!" she murmured. "What would he do without his music?"

The horses slowed down to a walk, and as they thundered over a rickety bridge, a scratching of the dry stones beneath startled them. Rearing, they brought the driver to his feet, whip raised over their backs.

"What, ho! What is this? What have we here?"

Fanny peered over the edge of the carriage. There, on his pony, hair on end, sat Peter!

"I–I thought you might like me to go home with you, Fanny," he began slowly. "Perhaps–perhaps you might be lonely without me."

Fanny looked into the eager, smudged young face. Winking back the tears, she put her hand on the narrow shoulder.

"Yes, Peter. But the others at home would be even more lonely if you did not go back to them. Besides, there are boys in my own country of France who need me now more than you. Surely you would not keep me from them."

Suddenly she smiled brightly.

"You will ride just over the hill with me. Then you will go back to Votkinsk."

When they reached the stopping place, she turned to him briskly.

"It is time now. Remember, Peter, I will write you little letters, and you will answer and let me know what you are doing with your music. Perhaps you will even write a composition for your own Fanny some day."

She took the small box from her pocket and slipped it into his hand.

"Do not open it until you are far beyond the little bridge," she directed. "Now we will play the game. Ready? Backs, turn! One, two, three."

Without another word she swept away to the carriage that would take her on to the next station. Turning slowly, Peter climbed up with the driver, ready to begin the journey back to Votkinsk.

"On with you, sleepyheads!" shouted the coachman, cracking the whip high in air. "No supper till you've earned it, back in the courtyard!"

The clopping hooves echoed along the dusty roadway. Looking back, Fanny watched her favorite pupil waving a grimy hand, while the other wiped hard at his eyes.

CHAPTER THREE

The moon, just slipping off to bed, turned a watchful eye on the Tchaikovskys, big and little, as they hurried from the house into the dim courtyard. Arms laden with belongings, they had a difficult time climbing into the two large carriages.

"I'm going to sit next to Peter, because he's the most fun," declared Nicholas. Squeezing and pushing, he was making himself a place beside his younger brother when the cousins sprang to the carriage steps.

"It's my turn to be next to Peter! No, mine! Mine!" they shouted.

The noise was deafening until Ilya loomed over their heads, shaking a warning finger at the scrambling heap.

"Another word," he scolded, "and you shall all ride atop the baggage!"

This was punishment, indeed, bringing instant silence.

"Now then," Ilya went on, "someone will need to sit in the lead carriage, to spell the driver on the hills. Petia has been the most patient," he decided briskly. "He shall have the place of honor."

In the twinkling of an eye, Peter climbed to the high seat behind the four spirited horses. For the first time, a little smile twisted the corners of his mouth. Old Sultan looked down at him closely.

"There'll be plenty for you to do in guiding the critters over the slippery places. A frisky lot this mornin', too."

"I can handle Lightfoot, even on ice," ventured Peter in a small voice. "So we won't have any trouble at all."

The old driver nodded. "Not until we get into Moscow, young 'un. Good to have a look at that fine city again."

A sudden command from Ilya started the carriage wheels grinding on the cobbles.

"We're off!"

"We're off! We're off!" echoed the children. With merry calling and hand waving, out of the courtyard they wheeled onto the road leading to Moscow.

This was a great adventure, and Peter felt like laughing and crying at the same time. But no one could be sad for long, with such gay shouting from the carriage behind.

"Mind the reins, young'un!" warned old Sultan. "Pull the lazy critters into line there, on the left."

Peter tugged hard on the stout leather bands and found himself making up a little jingle as they rolled along. Mother Tchaikovsky nodded at her husband and smiled.

"I pray that all will be well with our young singer," she sighed. Listening for a moment to the bright melody, she joined in the refrain with the children.

The hours sped by on wings, with snow sifting down from heavy skies. Peter's heart thumped for joy when they changed into sleighs, and the shining runners slid like magic through the white drifts. He listened happily to the music of the troika bells on the harnesses as they jingled along.

As they neared the city, more and more sleigh bells rang through the powdery mist, until the air was filled with delicate tinkling sounds.

"Hark!" Peter cried, waving his arms in a circle. "All the fairies in the world have come out to dance! Can't you hear them? They're going to the wedding of the snow queen!"

The old coachman looked down into the blue eyes, glowing like stars in the early dusk.

Lights appeared in the windows of the great houses, and watchdogs guarding the courtyards barked a warning to strangers. As they entered the city of Moscow, the chimes from a hundred church steeples clanged a salute to the night. The glory of sound was almost too much for Peter. He sprang from his place, hair standing on end.

"Steady, there! Steady, young'un!" Sultan hung onto the short coattail and pulled his young charge back under the heavy fur robe. "A right hearty welcome to the city of Moscow, eh?"

Peter shivered with joy, his eyes watching the twinkling lights, his ears filled with the music of the chimes and jingling troika bells. Never would he forget this night.

The days in the big city were exciting, indeed, filled to overflowing with strange sights and sounds. Then one evening, father Tchaikovsky announced sadly, "We must go on to St. Petersburg and find a new home. The position that I had hoped to find, is not here."

"My city!" cried Peter. "We are going to Petersburg!"

Another new adventure was at hand. Again the boxes and bundles were stored in the sleighs, and in a very short time, indeed, he found himself in snug, warm rooms in the big city of St. Petersburg.

But being indoors did not interest him for long. More and more he missed the open fields and roads and large courtyards with the animals at Votkinsk. At night he dreamed of his pony, Lightfoot, and wakened with a lump in his throat.

Crawling out of bed one morning very early, he decided it was time for adventure. A little exploring would be fun. Dressing quickly, he slipped down the stairs. A thick fog hung over the streets, and rounding a corner, he heard voices and the wailing of a cat cutting through the mist.

The animal was in pain! Peter's feet took wings. If only the fog would lift so that he could find the little creature.

Suddenly, in a little clearing, he came upon a group of older boys tying a cord around the body of a small black cat. As it twisted and turned, mewing and striking out with its claws to free itself, the boys shouted with laughter.

"Take that, and that!" cried a tall lad, bringing his fist down on the small, dark head.

Peter could not bear the horrible sight. In a rage he darted into the circle, his eyes flashing, arm in air.

"Stop!" he shouted, his voice trembling with anger. "Don't touch that poor little cat again!"

A fresh burst of laughter greeted his words.

"Can't save him now, fairhead," taunted the leader. "He'll be dead before you can count seven."

Peter's eyes narrowed. Taking a deep breath, he stepped swiftly to the thick-lipped boy, his face white.

"See, he is afraid, poor little animal. Please let me have him. I will take him home and you will never be bothered with him again," he begged.

The boys listened for a moment. Then, turning their backs, they tightened the cord until the cries of the cat rang out sharply. Peter could bear it no longer, and rushing at the group, he snatched the little animal from the startled leader.

"The cat is mine!" he shouted, holding the trembling creature against his neck. "If you touch him again, God will strike you dead!"

Turning, he darted off in the fog, the angry voices of the boys following close behind.

"Get him! Get that beggar! We'll teach him a lesson he'll never forget!"

Like an arrow Peter fled along the street. Stopping in an alleyway to rest, he crouched against the stone wall, scarcely

breathing lest the boys find his hiding place. Wrapping the black cat tenderly inside his coat, he whispered comforting words in his pink ear.

"There now, small one, you are safe. No need to tremble. They will never hurt you again."

When the sounds had died away, he crept from his hiding place and swiftly found his way home. As the door closed behind him, his mother looked up from her reading.

"A strange cat!" she exclaimed, putting her book down quickly. "Open the door and let him go at once, child!"

A look of fear crossed Peter's face, and he put the little animal back inside his coat.

"But I just saved his life, Mother! He's mine, forever! I'll call him Midnight."

Alexandra Tchaikovsky sighed and went back to her reading.

"Ah well, you may keep him for a time. Perhaps no harm will come of it."

Peter was as happy as he could be with his new pet, Midnight, following him wherever he went. But never did he allow the little animal to be out of his sight, fearing lest some harm should come to it. His greatest joy was to turn on his

beloved orchestrion at twilight. Sitting beside the instrument, he listened with all his might, Midnight curled in a round black ball on his shoulder, fast asleep.

Ilya, coming upon the pair one evening, said quietly, "Could you leave your pet long enough to hear a real orchestra in the theatre?"

Peter leaped to his feet, startling Midnight out of his wits.

"Oh Father!" He shouted, "To see real instruments and hear them all sounding together?"

"Yes, Petia. You will enjoy watching the men, and the leader, as well. Tomorrow we will go."

All the next day, Peter counted the hours until darkness fell over the city. At last, in his best suit and with his hair brushed until it shone, he set out for the music hall.

His first concert! Mother and father Tchaikovsky smiled as Peter leaned hard against the seat before him, waiting for the music to begin. Solemnly he watched as the men took their places on the platform, each carrying an instrument. Last of all came the conductor, and Peter clapped with all his might.

But when the lights were lowered and the music began, he could scarcely contain himself. The glory of sound flowed through him and seemed to carry him far away to another world.

He must get nearer the music. Without making the least noise, he slipped to the floor and in the darkness, crept on hands and knees down the aisle. The stage at last! Now he was a part of the music. He sat crouched against the boards, his eyes on the instruments, his breath coming short and fast.

His heart beat hard against his chest when the violins played the melody alone. The sad, sweet music made him want to shout and weep at the same moment. Never had he dreamed of anything so beautiful, his whole life long.

All the way home, his feet seemed scarcely to touch the ground, and his head felt light, as if it were floating in the air above him.

"You liked the music, son?" his father and mother asked again and again. But the only answer was a tight squeeze of the hand. One look at the shining face told them all.

That night Peter could not sleep, and the next day his eyes were heavy and the food on his plate was untouched. All that he could think about was the music of the orchestra.

"We will hear another concert soon?" he asked every hour, a faraway look in his eyes.

Kind mother Tchaikovsky sighed and patted the fair head, near her own. "Then you love music so much that you would give up everything in the world for it?"

Peter's face was like a sunray.

"Oh yes!" he cried, throwing his arms around his mother in a warm hug. "Music more than anything in all the whole wide world!"

Ilya came into the room, shaking a playful finger.

"There are other things in the whole wide world besides music, son. There are lessons. A good thing that tomorrow you and your brother will begin to know what real work is like in a large boys' school."

Poor Peter. Never could he have dreamed what was in store for him.

Early the next morning, his clothes all neatly packed, he buttoned himself into his heavy coat and stood at the door with his father and Nicholas, ready to leave. His mother straightened his cap and smiled a little sadly.

"Do all that the masters tell you, and work hard so that we will be proud of you, my son."

Off rode the three in the sleigh, the bells on the harness making a merry sound in the frosty air. Peter sat on the

outside, carefully keeping one hand in his large coat pocket. By now, Midnight was well used to traveling in the warm darkness, and purred contentedly against his master's hand.

Arriving at the school, the boys were taken at once to the housekeeper.

"Two new scalawags and more work for me," grumbled the tall, thin woman in black, fingering a heavy chain of keys at her belt. "Better not be mischief makers, or I'll know about it, soon enough!"

Ilya laughed at the solemn young faces.

"They're pretty good boys, and should give you no trouble," said he, lightly. "I will look in on them in a few weeks to see that all is well."

He was gone, and Peter and Nicholas roamed about the grounds, looking over the new quarters. A group of boys stopped playing, and their leader sauntered to meet them.

"What's your name, puddin' head?" he shouted, planting a hard fist in Peter's side.

At the sharp cry of pain, Nicholas flew at the older student, his blows making short work of the bully who ran screaming for help.

There were whacks and thumps from other groups of boys through the rest of the day, and Nicholas looked fearfully at his younger brother.

"You'll have to stand up and fight, Petia!"

"Y–yes, Nicholas. This is the fightingest place I ever saw! Lucky they haven't touched Midnight."

Peter's hand patted the little creature snuggled against his side.

"They'll never let you keep him," declared Nicholas, startled at the sudden look of fear at his words.

"But he's so little, they'll never know I have him," objected Peter. "He'll always be in my pocket, and I'll save him scraps from my plate."

After a simple supper, the boys parted company and were soon in their narrow, hard cots. Peter felt lonely, indeed, on

his first night away from home. The icy chill crept into his very bones. Shivering, he crept far under the covers, burying Midnight with him.

"What would I ever do without you?" he whispered, running his hand over the round furry back. Comforted a little, he fell into a deep, troubled sleep.

A loud bell jangling through the hallways startled him from his bed the next morning. Down the cold, wide stairs he clumped with the smaller boys to breakfast of black bread and broth.

For four long hours there were lessons on hard benches, with sharp raps on knuckles if there were any mistakes. Poor Peter! A cold lunch in the dining hall, and the lessons went on steadily until sundown. Only a few minutes were allowed for play, with whackings from the boys, until a horrible bell called everyone to a meager supper of fish and bread and turnips.

Peter looked at the food on his plate and felt his stomach turn within him. How he longed for the good hot dishes at home that he liked so well. A hard lump swelled in his throat that he could not swallow.

"Aren't hungry? Then I'll eat it, lighthead," said the grimy boy at his side. There was just time to snatch the crust of bread for Midnight before the plate was emptied.

Lessons, lessons, lessons. Would they never end? Peter's head ached, and he felt hungry. Holding his head in his hands, he stared down at the numbers that seemed to jump at him from the page. Six and twenty-seven. Six and twenty-seven. Six and ... Peter's eyes began to close.

"Tchaikovsky! At work, young man! No lazy students here!"

Peter swallowed his tears. "Yes, sir! Yes, sir!" he mumbled, shaking himself awake.

Would the bell never ring? Just as he thought he could stand it no longer, CLANG! went the gong.

"Eight o'clock. Bedtime, young gentlemen."

Numb with the cold, Peter fell into bed without waiting to take off his clothes. With warm little Midnight held tight against his chest, he fell fast asleep. In his dreams, the teacher was running after him with a long rod. Down a narrow, white alley he was fleeing with all his might. Narrower and narrower it grew, and closer and closer came the stick over his back. Whack! He was caught!

His own shouting wakened him. How glad he was to see the daylight struggling through the blinds and hear the din of the rising bell. An endless morning dragged by. White and weary, as he was on his way to the lunch hall, he caught sight of his older brother.

"Nicholas, oh Nicholas, save me!" Peter's arms started to close round him while the hot tears began to fall.

Nicholas looked swiftly over his shoulder, his hand on Peter's arm.

"Quiet!" he cautioned in low tones. "If the boys hear you, they will make you miserable."

But Peter did not care.

"Oh Nicholas, let us go away from here!" he begged, tears

welling again in his eyes. "Let us go home, Nicholas!"

"But mother and father would think we were cowards."

At the words, Peter loosened his hold and swallowed hard. Slowly he followed the boys into the dining hall.

That night, just as he was crawling into bed, Midnight squirmed from his hand and fell with a soft little thud to the floor. Like a flash he whisked out of the door and down the hall.

Terror seized Peter, and he was after him in a second, calling softly, "Midnight! Midnight! Come, Midnight!" But he kept just ahead, his tail waving over his back.

There–he was stopping at a door! Lifting his paw, he scratched on it and mewed. Just as Peter pounced down on him a loud creak sounded, and there stood the housekeeper in long dressing gown, her bony finger pointing down at Midnight.

"Boy!" she gasped. "How did that pest get into this house?"

Peter was frozen in his tracks as the harsh face came nearer and nearer.

"Why—you see—he's mine! He's my own pet! He won't hurt anything, I promise. You can even borrow him sometime for the rats and mice, if you have any."

The words tumbled out in a stream as the cold eyes kept staring at him.

"Pets are not allowed in this house. The cat shall be turned out at once. If the masters find it around, you will feel the cane on your back, young scalawag. Off with you! To bed!"

The horrible words echoed in his ears as Peter crawled again under the covers. But much worse was the loss of his dearest companion.

"Midnight! Midnight!" Great sobs shook him as he hid his head in the pillow. On and on he wept for the little creature that had left him. When there were no more tears, he fell fast asleep, hunting through the town in his dreams for the warm, furry little animal.

When morning dawned, Peter was ill, indeed, and a woman in a white uniform was bending over him.

"Where do you feel badly, young man?" she questioned him briskly, poking at his eyes to make them stay open.

"Here," whispered Peter, pointing to his chest. "In here."

"Your father will arrive very soon."

New hope stirred within him, and with a little smile, Peter drifted again into the land of dreams. When he awoke, there, beside him, sat Ilya Tchaikovsky.

"No words, young man." His father smiled down at him. "Perhaps you would like to go home with me for a little visit. Oho! That pleases you so much? Then up with you, lad, and off we go."

Never was there a happier boy in all the great city. Back again in the warm, comfortable sitting room, with his loved ones close beside him, he talked until there were no more words.

"So quickly you are better, my son," said Ilya, gently. "Then a fine surprise there is for you, boy. But only if you promise to go quietly back to the school again."

At the look of pain, Ilya added quickly, "It is the opera, Petia, with beautiful music and singers in costume acting the story. And a fine orchestra there will be, to accompany the singers."

To hear instruments again! Peter leaped from his chair, his eyes glowing.

"Yes! I will go back to the school if I can hear the orchestra!"

A few nights later, as the heavenly music accompanied the best singers in all the city, Peter drank in the glory of sound and watched the beautiful scenes as if in a dream. His first opera in the city of St. Petersburg!

At home in his snug, warm bed, he lay awake through the hours, hugging himself with delight as the music danced in his head.

True to his promise, he went back to the school with Ilya.

"We must see that you begin lessons at once with the piano master," said father Tchaikovsky. "Who knows, perhaps the school work will go better with a little music."

The frail little teacher listened in surprise to the new pupil as his fingers flew over the keys.

"The boy should do well with such a good beginning. He is very far advanced for his years, sir."

But as the months rolled by, Peter did not work too hard at the piano. More and more he begged to go to concerts and operas and, after each performance, became more excited with the music that he had heard.

"He is too deeply moved by the sounds," said mother Tchaikovsky to her husband, as she watched the pale face of her son and the hollow eyes that told of no sleep.

One morning, after a lovely concert, Peter did not leave his bed. Quietly his mother laid her hand on the hot forehead and sent at once for the good doctor.

"Hm! Measles," said he. "No school for you for a time, young man." As the eyelids flickered at the words, he nodded wisely. "So! Measles are better than school!" he laughed.

But when the illness was finished, Peter still did not care to leave his warm bed.

"You must take the boy to the country," ordered the doctor. "Green meadows and fresh air should make the cheeks plump and rosy again."

Peter could hardly believe the good news. No more long white halls of the school. No more hard benches and cross teachers and lessons from morning until night.

"We will go away soon?" he questioned every day as soon as he opened his eyes. "And we will take the orchestrion with us!"

For the first time in many long months, he began to sing a new song of his own making:

"We're going to the country, the country, the country," he began. Then, with a burst of laughter at his own silly thoughts, he added, "We're going to the country, to get us pigs and hens!"

Off to the green meadows went the Tchaikovskys, this time to a very small mining town, even smaller than Votkinsk. Soon Ilya was at work again, and Peter was as happy as could be. Singing at the top of his lungs, he roamed about, his younger sister, Alexandra, and brother, Ipolyte, following him like little shadows.

But Peter hardly noticed them. Something strange was happening to him now. The whole world was turning to music. Everything around him spoke to him in melody. Giant trees bending over his head whispered their special songs as he passed under their sheltering arms. The river, racing over the rocks in the shallow bend, sparkled in clean, liquid tones. Bright patches of flowers, smiling up at him from the emerald grasses, greeted him in gentle rhythm.

Even the farmyard creatures in the early hours of the morning, chattered to him in such gay chorus that he squatted down beside them in peals of laughter, singing and whistling back at them. Then the big fat hens eyed him silently, standing

first on one leg, then on the other, heads cocked knowingly toward him.

"Peter!" The new governess pounced on him from behind, frightening him almost out of his wits. "The father and mother will be angry if we do not begin the lessons at once."

Indoors he followed her without a word. But no lessons would he do until he had covered sheets of his copybook with notes of the melodies that he had just heard. In a great stream they raced from his pen.

"Listen, Madame!" he exclaimed suddenly, rushing to the piano. "This is the lazy pig, scolding her husband. Now you needn't laugh!" He paused abruptly, hands raised over the keys, his blue eyes flashing. "I heard her with my own ears tell the swaggering one not to go gossiping with common pigs again.

Copybook after copybook of his dearest treasures Peter carefully locked away in an old chest, and carried the heavy key in his pocket. Only one beloved friend was to see them. Many of the little tunes he tucked into letters and sent off to France to his dear old Fanny. And never did she forget to answer him, scolding him gently if his lessons were not going too well. At her words, Peter would burst into a flood of tears and work with a fury at his books.

His greatest joy was to roam with a trusted servant into the countryside where he could hear the peasants singing at their work. Late one afternoon, on a lonely road leading back to the village, he stopped suddenly, finger in air.

"Violins! There must be a celebration!" he declared, racing off among the trees.

Leaping over fallen logs, he darted headlong into the underbrush, splashed through a shallow brook, and came at last to a little clearing. Soaked through and through and covered with mud and leaves, he stood trembling with joy at the scene that met his eyes.

Before a new little hut, a bride and groom were standing, country-folk dancing and singing in a circle around them. Three fiddlers in gay costume sawed away their jolly tunes for the merry company.

In a flash, Peter leaped into the whirling circle, clapping his hands and clicking his heels like the men. When the music stopped, he bowed to the happy couple and began to sing a

little song that he made up as he went along:

"Oh happy, happy, happy pair,
    You may know want, you may know care.
    But through your lives this day will be
    A mem'ry to eternity.
    Tra-la-la-la, Tra-la-la-la,
    A mem'ry to eternity."

At the tra-la-la's, the company and fiddlers joined in the refrain until the woods echoed with the new wedding song. At the end of the gay music, Peter suddenly looked around and, like a frightened rabbit, darted away as quickly as he had come.

Home through the woods he followed the servant, a faraway look in his eyes as the dancing tunes of the countryfolk wove themselves into a larger composition in his mind.

Through the long months Peter lived in his new world of music, until one afternoon when his father returned from work at the mines.

"Quite a young man you are becoming now," he declared, thoughtfully. "Time to be getting back to the big city and school again. Two years is long enough away."

But a big surprise was in store for Peter before he started on his way. Coming downstairs one morning, he was startled at the sound of a baby's cry. Following the noise, he looked cautiously into a low crib and discovered not one, but two new little brothers! Breathless with joy, he peered long at the squirming creatures, bundled snugly in blankets under the eagle eye of their nurse.

"My brothers, my own dear little brothers!" he breathed.

Every hour of the day he stole back to look at them and, in a frenzy of delight, raced off to the schoolroom to tell his beloved friend the glorious news. His pen flew over the paper.

"Dear Fanny,

I will give you the surprise of your life! You cannot guess what has come in the night. Two tiny new brothers. Yes, they are twins. I go to peek at them often. They are little angels come down from heaven. They do not seem real at all. Any minute I think they may fly away into the sky to be at home again. I love them so much. And Mother seems quite beside herself with joy. She is more beautiful than ever."

Sadly, Peter went back to the big city and was soon settled in school. But very lonely he was, and his thoughts turned again and again to the dear little brothers, Anatole and Modeste, that he had left behind. Eagerly he watched for mail, and hungrily read of their doings.

"Dear Petia," wrote his mother.

"You would scarcely know your small brothers. They have grown very tall and are into every kind of mischief. Only this morning, when the cook searched for her butter cask, she found her precious butter dumped onto the floor, and seven baby ducks swimming in the cask! And your dog has been hiding most of the time since they dressed him in tight clothes last week. But that is not all. They hitched him to the pony cart and made him pull them all the way to the village and back in such a costume. Poor Trigger has not been the same, since."

At last Mother and Father Tchaikovsky decided to return to St. Petersburg to live. Peter could scarcely contain himself for joy, now that he could spend the weekends at home. School was not quite so horrible, with his lovely mother to listen to all his troubles. And the twins! Peter would not let them out of his sight.

"Come, my frisky colts, you shall spend the whole day with your big brother," he would promise them. Then what gay times they had together.

But the most terrible day in all their lives was when a dreadful sickness carried lovely Mother Tchaikovsky far away from the earth. Peter was in a daze. Never to see her beautiful face again? And never to hear her comforting voice when all the world was wrong? And worst of all, his little four-year-old brothers would have no mother to look after them.

Peter felt the hot tears all over again as he looked into the forlorn little faces. Throwing his arms around the small shoulders, he held them close, and the three clung together, weeping as though their hearts would break.

"Never mind, my dears," he comforted them. "I will take care of you now, and nothing will ever harm you."

From that time on, no music came from Peter. Not a single note went down in the copybook, and his piano was silent. Only to Fanny did he pour out his troubles in little letters.

> "I do not play my piano now," he wrote. "Excepting now and then when I am alone, just to comfort myself a little."

More and more of his time Peter spent with the twins, and Ilya smiled as he listened to the voices at bedtime.

"Kolia, the ears are not yet clean. And remember, no stories until you are quietly in bed. Come, Anatole, I will teach you how to bow properly, so that you can grow up like a gentleman."

At last the voices were stilled, and as Peter crept from the darkened room, his father met him with arm outstretched.

"How good you are to the little boys," he declared. "A great comfort, Petia." He was silent for a moment. "If only your school reports were as comforting, my son, I would be more content."

Peter broke in hurriedly, his fists clenched.

"I cannot bear the studies, father!" he cried. "They are so difficult, and my heart is not in them." Suddenly a light smile flitted over his handsome face. "If you would allow me, sir, I would gladly stay at home and look after the little boys all day long. Or music—I would work hard at it, father."

Ilya shook his head. "No, no, that would never do! You must keep on at the school, and before we know it, you will make us very proud, indeed, when we address you as *Lawyer Peter Tchaikovsky!*"

A great loneliness settled over Peter. How could anyone know of the music that was burning in his mind, calling out to him through the long hours of the day and night? In his heart he held his precious treasure for ten long years, where none might see.

He would have been startled if he could know of the strange happening that was to unlock the doors and let the river of melody go racing on, never to end.

Little did Peter know, on that cold, frosty night, that the little Russian boy from the tiny mining town of Votkinsk, would one day be honored round the whole world for his glowing, singing melodies, the melodies of Peter Ilyich Tchaikovsky.

Here are some of the bright melodies that came from the pen of Peter Tchaikovsky. They will bring you great joy when you have learned to play them.

ITALIAN SONG

Moderato

THE ORGAN-GRINDER

Moderato

FRENCH SONG

Andantino

MAZURKA

Allegro

106

KAMARINSKAJA
Russian Dance

Allegro

108

YODEL SONG

Moderato

112

AT CHURCH

Andantino

The Story of Peter Tchaikovsky is part of *Music Appreciation: Book 2 for the Middle Grades*.

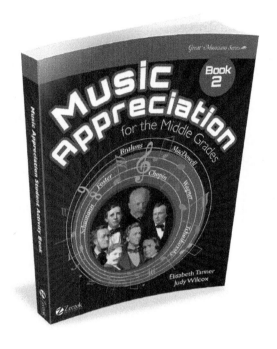

Music Appreciation: Book 2 for the Middle Grades (for grades 5 to 8) will introduce older children to seven different composers, dating from 1810 to 1908 (Chopin, Schumann, Wagner, Foster, Brahms, Tchaikovsky and MacDowell). Each composer's childhood and adult life are vividly described in individual biographies. Every important incident is mentioned and every detail of the stories is true. Each book contains written music and delightful pictures throughout. It is more than the human side of these books that will make them live, for in the music the great masters breathe.

The Student Book incorporates activities from across the curriculum and promotes an increased knowledge of and appreciation for classical music and the composers. Geared for a variety of learners—auditory, kinesthetic, visual, and just plain "active"—it is user-friendly for multi-age groups.

<u>Titles used in this curriculum are:</u>
Frederic Chopin, Early Years
Frederic Chopin, Later Years
Robert Schumann and Mascot Ziff
Adventures of Richard Wagner
Stephen Foster and His Little Dog Tray
The Young Brahms
The Story of Peter Tchaikovsky
Peter Tchaikovsky and the Nutcracker Ballet
Edward MacDowell and His Cabin in the Pines

For more information visit our website at www.Zeezok.com

Also available from Zeezok Publishing:

Music Appreciation: Book 1 for the Elementary Grades (for grades 1 to 6) will introduce children to seven different composers, dating from 1685 to 1828 (Bach, Handel, Haydn, Mozart, Beethoven, Paganini and Schubert). Each composer's childhood and adult life are vividly described in individual biographies. Every important incident is mentioned and every detail of the stories is true. Each book contains written music and delightful pictures throughout. It is more than the human side of these books that will make them live, for in the music the great masters breathe.

The Student Activity book includes a variety of hands-on activities such as: geography lessons, history lessons, recipes, instrument studies, music vocabulary, hand writing, musical facts of the Classical period, timelines, character trait studies, and so much more. Geared for a variety of learners— auditory, kinesthetic, visual, and just plain "active"—the Student Activity Book is an excellent companion to your reading experience.

Titles used in this curriculum are:
Sebastian Bach, The Boy from Thuringia
Handel at the Court of Kings
Joseph Haydn, The Merry Little Peasant
Mozart, The Wonder Boy
Ludwig Beethoven and the Chiming Tower Bells
Paganini, Master of Strings
Franz Schubert and His Merry Friends

For more information visit our website at www.Zeezok.com